ISBN 978-1-331-90760-2
PIBN 10252484

This book is a reproduction of an important historical work. Forgotten Books uses
state-of-the-art technology to digitally reconstruct the work, preserving the original format
whilst repairing imperfections present in the aged copy. In rare cases, an imperfection in
the original, such as a blemish or missing page, may be replicated in our edition. We do,
however, repair the vast majority of imperfections successfully; any imperfections that
remain are intentionally left to preserve the state of such historical works.

1 MONTH OF
FREE
READING

at

www.ForgottenBooks.com

By purchasing this book you are eligible for one month membership to ForgottenBooks.com, giving you unlimited access to our entire collection of over 700,000 titles via our web site and mobile apps.

To claim your free month visit:

www.forgottenbooks.com/free252484

Similar Books Are Available from
www.forgottenbooks.com

MEMOIR

OF THE DISTINGUISHED MOHAWK
INDIAN CHIEF, SACHEM
AND WARRIOR,

CAPT. JOSEPH BRANT

COMPILED FROM THE MOST

RELIABLE AND AUTHENTIC RECORDS.

INCLUDING A BRIEF HISTORY OF
THE PRINCIPAL EVENTS
OF HIS LIFE, WITH
AN APPENDIX.

AND PORTRAIT

BRANTFORD, ONTARIO:

C. E. STEWART & CO , BOOK AND JOB PRINTERS, GEORGE STREET

1872.

CONTENTS.

CHAPTER I.

THAYENDANEGEA, born on the Ohio River, youngest son of Nickus Brant—Joins the expedition of Gen. Wm. Johnson against Niagara—Is sent to Moore's School at Lebanon, Conn. Letter of Sir Wm. Johnson—Returns from school—Is employed by the Rev. Charles Jeffrey Smith as Interpreter and Assistant Joins the Indian forces in the Pontiac War .. ..Page 7

CHAPTER II.

Capture of Fort Niagara by the forces under Generel (afterwards Sir Wm.) Johnson—Desertion of the Western Indians of the French cause—They join the Six Nations—Sir Wm. Johnson takes Molly Brant as his wife, or housekeeper, and appoints Joseph Brant to office in tne Indian Department—Death of Sir William Johnson—Col. Guy Johnson succeeds to his office of Superintendent of Indian affairs—He appoints Joseph Brant his Secretary—Brant's first marriage..... Page 13

CHAPTER III.

Revolutionary spirit in the Mohawk Valley—The Mohawks join the English—Joseph Brant becomes the leader of the Indian forces—Col. Johnson compelled to leave the Mohawk Valley—Retreats to Montreal with Brant at the head of two hundred and twenty Indian Warriors, by way of Lake Ontario —Brant goes to England with Col. Johnson— Much noticed in London— Makes a speech—Returns to New York and is dispatched with a message to the Six Nations--- Joins the expedition of Gen. Saint Leger against Fort Stanwix, with three hundred Warriors of the Six Nations—Indians suffer severely in an engagement—Depredations upon the Oneidas—Molly Brant and her children flee to the Onondagas— She gives valuable information to Gen. St. Leger— Brant forms an ambush and nearly destroys the force of the American Gen. Herkimer—Col. Claus compliments Brant at Niagara— Brant offers to join the forces of Sir William Howe......Page 19

CHAPTER IV.

Col. Guy Johnson suggests the plan of employing the Indians in a " *Petit Guerre*"—Expedition against Wyoming--Campbell's Poem, " Gertrude of Wyoming"—John Brant visits the Poet, who retracts certain statements in regard to his father
....Page 25

CHAPTER V.

Brant's humanity at Cherry Valley—Difficulty in subsisting the loyal forces in the field—The means resorted to to obtain provisions—Letter of Joseph Brant........................ ..Page 29

CHAPTER VI.

Gen. Sullivan's campaign against the Senecas opposed by the whole British forces—Brant in command of the Indians—His distinguished valor and military skill on the occasion—Saves the life of Lieut. Boyd, taken prisoner by the Indians—Severity of the winter of 1779-80—Capt. Wm. Powell marries Miss Moore, one of the Cherry Valley prisoners—Capt. Brant being present is married to his third wife, after the form of the English Church—Heads an expedition from Niagara into the Mohawk Valley—Capture of Capt. Harper, who is taken to Niagara a prisoner by the Indians—His life saved through the instrumentality of Brant and Capt. Wm. Powell—Capture of Capt. Jeremiah Snider—His description of Fort Niagara and its officers.... ....Page 35

CHAPTER VII.

Peace between Great Britain and the United States declared 1783—The Mohawks flee to Canada, residing temporarily on the eastern side of the Niagara River—A tract of land on the Bay of Quinte offered them—A tract of land on the Grand River was preferred—Brant visits England..................Page 45

CHAPTER VIII.

Brant accompanies the expedition against Gen. St. Clair, who is defeated near Pittsburgh—Brant's influence sought and his ability acknowledged by the United States—He visits Philadelphia—Notices of the visit by the newspapers—A change in the Government of Canada—Difference in regard to the interpretation of the title to their lands on the Grand River—Erection of a Church on their Reservation—Brant's speech at Niagara in regard to their lands............... ... ...Page 55

CHAPTER IX.

Brant's correspondence in respect to their lands and the settlement of a Missionary among his people—His wives and children –Death of his oldest son by the hands of his father —The education of his children—His correspondence in relation thereto—Removes to the head of Lake Ontario—Builds a dwelling there—His death, &c., &c.... ....Page 63

INTRODUCTION.

After the lapse of more than half a century since the death of the famous Indian Chief and Warrior, Captain Joseph Brant, it is thought that a brief history of his life, character and exploits, in a cheap and popular form, would be acceptable to the British public, particularly that of the Dominion of Canada.

The following memoir has been carefully compiled from the most reliable sources, and may be considered entirely authentic.

Much has been written about the distinguished Chief of the Mohawks, who, perhaps, in all the phases of his character, was the most celebrated of all the Aborigines who have distinguished themselves in the eyes of Europeans on this continent since the work of civilization began. But in general his history has been so mixed up with that of contemporaneous events, that without access to extensive libraries of books, and an intelligent and careful study and comparison of impartial authorities, a true index to the character and acts of Capt. Joseph Brant was impossible. In this brief memoir the proper mean between the two extremes, of too much praise or too much blame, has been attempted, and, it is believed, measurably attained.

BRANTFORD, Ontario, July, 1872.

MEMOIR

OF

CAPT. JOSEPH BRANT.

CHAPTER I.

"Thayendanegea," or Joseph Brant, as he was called in English, according to tradition, was born on the banks of the "Belle," or beautiful river, according to the French, or "Oh-he-oh," according to the Indian vocabulary, about the year 1742.

He was the youngest son of a distinguished Mohawk Chief, mentioned in various records and traditions, under the

English or German name of "Niekus Brant," between whom and Sir William Johnson it is said a close intimacy subsisted. Three sons of "Niekus Brant" accompanied the expedition against Crown Point in 1755, which was commanded by Gen. Wm. Johnson. Joseph was the younger of the three, and could not have been over 13 or 14 years of age at that time.

This expedition was successful, and procured for Sir Wm. Johnson his title of Baronet, and a gratuity of five thousand pounds from the King. Gen. Johnson observing the promising qualities of the boy, procured for him a place in Moore's Charity School, opened by the Rev. Dr. Wheelock, of Lebanon, Conn.

The following letter of Sir William Johnson's, sufficiently illustrates his views in regard to the education of the Indians at this time:

FORT JOHNSON, }
Nov. 17th, 1761.}

REV. SIR :

Yours of the second instant I had
the pleasure of receiving by the hands of
Mr. Kirkland. I am pleased to find the
lads I sent have merited your good
opinion of them. I have given it in
charge to Joseph (Brant) to speak in my
name to any good boys he may see, and
encourage them to accept the generous
offers now made them, which he promises
to do, and return as soon as possible. I
will, on return of the Indians from hunting, advise them to send as many as is
required. I expect they will return, and
hope they will make such progress in the
English language, and their learning, as
may prove to your satisfaction and the
benefit of those who are really much to be
pitied. My absence these four months
has prevented my design of encouraging
some more lads going to you, and since
my return, which is but lately, I have not
had an opportunity of seeing old or young,

being all on their hunt.   When they come back I shall talk and advise their parents to embrace this favorable opportunity of having their children instructed, and doubt not of their readiness to lay hold of so kind and charitable an affair.

Mr. Kirkland's intention of learning the Mohawk language I most approve of, as after acquiring it, he could be of vast service to them as a clergyman, which they much want and are desirous of having.

The present laudable design of instructing a number of Indian boys will, I doubt not, when more known, lead several gentlemen to contribute towards it, and enable you thereby to increase the number of schollars, with whom I shall not be backward to contribute my mite.

I wish you all success in this undertaking, and am with truth and sincerity,

Rev. Sir,

Your most humble servant,

WM. JOHNSON.

The Moore's Charity School was established with the philanthropic design of educating Indian boys, and was continued for a length of time, but with indifferent success, so far as the original object was concerned.

It was originated and principally supported by the patronage of English philanthropists, where " Joseph" remained a sufficient time to acquire some knowledge of the English language, and of reading and writing.

The confinement proved irksome to him, however, and he soon returned to his native home and pursuits. On his return from school, Joseph was employed by Sir William Johnson in public business, particularly that relating to the Indians. He was also employed by the Rev. Charles Jeffrey Smith, a missionary to the Indians, as an interpreter and assistant, in which he exhibited both zeal and effi-

ciency.   The Pontiac War breaking out
about this time, he left his studies and
joined the forces as an officer, and was
active in the war, " in which he behaved
so much like the Christian and soldier,
that he gained great esteem."

CHAPTER II.

The expedition against Niagara in 1759, which was then in possession of the French, was organized under the command of Gen. Prideaux, consisting of a little over two thousand men, left Oswego for Niagara, 1st September, of that year. Sir William Johnson joined the expedition with about six hundred warriors of the Six Nations. This number was increased to about one thousand before reaching the vicinity of the Fort. The youthful warrior accompanied Sir William in this expedition. The French had drawn all their available forces of every description from their western posts for the defence of Niagara.

A large detachment arrived in the vicinity during . the siege, consisting of both French and Indians. These Indians were friends and allies of the Six Nations. A parley between the Indians was held. The Western Indians declaring they did not come to fight their brethren of the Six Nations, but the English.

The result was they detached themselves and joined their brethren. In the early part of the siege Gen. Prideaux was killed by the accidental discharge of a " cohorn," and the command devolved upon Sir William Johnson. Upon the withdrawal of the Western Indians, the French were attacked, and all either killed, taken prisoners, or put to flight.

Upon learning the fate of this reinforcement, the French commandant surrendered the Fort, himself, and all his forces prisoners of war. On the death of

Lady Johnson, Sir William took to his home " Miss Molly" as she was called, the daughter of his distinguished friend " Nickus Brant," sister of Joseph Brant, as his wife, which proved to be a judicious choice and a happy union. This circumstance contributed greatly to the advance ment of her young brother, who resided with the family of Sir William, and he was appointed to office by him in the Indian Department.

The first mutterings of discontent of the American Colonists against the parent government of Great Britain, found our young hero just merging into manhood.

He was allied to the leader and representative of the Crown in the Mohawk Valley, and henceforward acted with him up to the time of Sir William's death, which occurred suddenly in June, 1774. Col. Guy Johnson, the nephew of Sir

William, and also son-in-law, by virtue of marrying his daughter, succeeded to his office as Superintendent of the Six Nations of Indians, and appointed Joseph Brant his secretary. Joseph Brant was married quite young, probably about 1767. His first wife was the daughter of a Chief of the Oneidas. By her he had two children, a son and a daughter. On the death of this wife, which occurred about 1771 or 2, he resumed his studies under Rev. Dr. Stewart at Fort Hunter, who was then engaged in a revision of the translation of the Prayer Book and portions of the Scriptures into the Mohawk language, in which Joseph was of great assistance to him. It is stated that during this sojourn with the Rev. Dr. Stewart, Brant applied to the Dr. to marry him to the sister of his deceased wife ; but the service was declined on account of the " forbidden re-

lationship." But the ceremony was subsequently performed by a less scrupulous
German Ecclesiastic. It was about this
period that Brant became the subject of
serious religious impressions, attaching
himself to the English Church, of which
he continued a member until his death.

CHAPTER III.

The discontent of the Colonists which had hitherto been confined to Boston and the New England Colonies, now began to manifest itself in the Mohawk Valley The Johnsons and other loyalists in the Valley, were active in counteracting the revolutionary spirit, which led to great excitement and nearly culminated in open hostilities between the opposing parties. Of course the Mohawks sympathized with their friends the English, and Joseph Brant, almost by force of circumstances, became the military leader of the loyal Indians, who constituted a majority of the military force with which the loyalists took the field. The vigorous measures of

the Colonists soon compelled Col. Johnson to leave the Mohawk Valley for Cana
da He arrived in Montreal July 14th,
1775, accompanied by Joseph Brant with
two hundred and twenty Indians, by way
of Lake Ontario, expecting soon to orga-
nize a force sufficient to return and take
possession of the homes and property he
and his retainers had left behind. But,
failing in these endeavors, and finding
his official standing and powers were
interfered with to some extent, by
the appointment of Major Campbell as
Indian Agent for Canada, Col. Johnson
decided to go to England to get the
question of his powers and jurisdiction
settled.

He proceeded to Quebec and sailed
for England, November 11th, taking
Joseph Brant and a Mohawk War Chief
named Oteroughyanente with him. Brant
was much noticed and courted in London,

and made a speech before Lord George Germain, setting forth the grievances of the Six Nations in general, and of the Mohawks, his own nation, in particular. To which Lord Germain made a brief reply. This speech, which is the first of Brant's we have on record, seems to have been delivered in London, March, 1776.

The sojourn of Col. Johnson, with his Indian deputies, in England appears to have been short, as they arrived in New York on their return, July 29th, of the following year.

Soon after their return to New York, Joseph Brant was dispatched by Col. Johnson to the Six Nations with a message, and returned with their answer, saying " they were all ready to engage in the service, except the Oneidas, and ready to join Gen. Howe's army, and to act as one man."

The next we hear of Brant is at the head of three hundred warriors at Oswego, 1777, to join the expedition of Gen. St. Leger against Fort Stanwix. The Indians under Brant met with a severe loss in an engagement, and on their way home, committed some depredations upon the Oneidas, whom they considered rebels for their refusal to join the expedition. In retaliation, the Oneidas plundered Brant's sister, " Molly Brant", who resided with her family at the Upper Mohawk Town, together with others of the Mohawks who accompanied Brant in this expedition.

"Molly Brant" and her family fled to the Onondagas, the council-place of the Six Nations, and laid her grievances before that body. The information given to Gen. St. Leger of the approach of the reinforce ments of the rebels under Gen. Herkimer, was through the instrumentality of "Molly

Brant," and led to the surprise and almost defeat of the entire party under Gen. Herkimer Capt. Brant with a strong force of Indians, with true Indian sagacity, formed an ambuscade in a position admirably fitted for the purpose. The whole rebel army, with the exception of the rear guard, fell into the trap, and would have been destroyed had not a severe storm of thunder, lightning and rain, put a stop to the work of death. Col. Claus in a letter to Secretary Cox, dated, November 6th, 1777, compliments Joseph Brant for his distinguished services, and that of his party on this occasion. In November, 1777, Cols. Bolton and Butler wrote to Sir William Howe from Niagara, that Joseph Brant was there, and with themselves, waiting his orders, wishing to know when and where they can be of use, saying they only wish to know the time and place, as they were confident of being well supported.

CHAPTER IV

Early in 1778 Col. Guy Johnson writing to Lord Germain from New York suggests the plan of employing the Indians in a " *Petit Guerre*" in their own way. The first expedition under this new mode of warfare was organized at Niagara under Col. John Butler, consisting of Loyalists and Indians, and was directed against Wyoming. In after years a poem entitled " Gertrude of Wyoming," written by Campbell, the Poet, made Brant the leader in this expedition, and heaped great obloquy upon his good name and character, for his

more than savage barbarity on that occasion; whereas, he was not present. This
was abundantly and satisfactorily proved
by his son John Brant, while on a visit to
the Poet, who promised to retract the
statement, which he did in the next
edition of his work, soon after published.*

---

* I took the character of Brant in the Poem of "Gertrude
of Wyoming," from the commmon histories of England; all of
which represented him as a bloody and bad man even among
savages, and chief agent in the horrible desolation of
Wyoming.

Some years after this poem appeared, the son of Brant, a
most interesting and intelligent youth, came over to England,
and I formed an acquaintance with him, on which I still look
back with pleasure. He appealed to my sense of honor and
justice, on his own part and that of his sister, to retract the
unfair aspersions, which, unconscious of their unfairness, I
had cast on his father's memory. He then referred me to
documents which completely satisfied me that the common
accounts of Brant's cruelties at Wyoming, which I found in
books of travels, and in Adolpus's and similar histories of
England, were gross errors, and that in point of fact, Brant
was not even present at that scene of desolation. It is, un-
happily, to Britons and Anglo-Americans that we must refer

the chief blame in this horrible business. I published a letter expressing this belief in the *New Monthly Magzine*, in the year 1822, to which I must refer the reader if he has any curiosity on the subject, for an antidote to my fanciful description of Brant. Among other expressions to young Brant, I made use of the following words: Had I learned all this of your father, when I was writing my poem, he should not have figured in it as the hero of mischief.

It was but bare justice to say thus much of a Mohawk Indian who spoke English eloquently, and was thought capable of having written a history of the Six Nations. I also learned that he often strove to mitigate the cruelty of Indian warfare. The name of Brant, therefore, remains in my poem a *pure* and *declared* character of *fiction.—Campbell.*

CHAPTER V

Brant's humanity was conspicuously displayed the same year in the attack upon Cherry Valley, at which he *was* present, but was not in command.

This expedition, too, was organized at Niagara, at the instigation of Walter Butler, son of Col. John Butler, and was placed under command of Walter Butler. Capt. Brant, who, with his Indian warriors, had been employed on the Susquehanna during most of the summer, was on his return to winter quarters at Niagara. Meeting Butler with his forces, bearing an order for Brant to join the expedition with his force. Brant was reluctant to do so, displeased at being placed under command of Walter Butler; but he was too much a soldier to refuse to obey orders. History has recorded to the credit of Joseph Brant that on this occasion he exhibited traits of humanity which seemed to be wanting in *some* at least of the white men present. "In a house which he entered he found a woman engaged in her usual avocations, 'Why are you thus engaged?' said Brant to her, 'while your neighbors are being murdered all around you?' 'We are king's people," she replied. 'That plea will not avail you to-day. They have murdered Mr. Well's family who are as dear to me as my own.' 'There is one Joseph Brant,' she said, 'if he is with the Indians he will save us.' 'I am Joseph Brant,' said he, 'but I have not the command, and I know not whether I can save you. But I will do what I can.' While speaking, several Seneca's were observed approaching the house. 'Get into bed and feign yourself sick,' said Brant, hastily. When the Senecas came in, he told them there was no person there but a sick woman and her children, and besought them to leave the house, which after a short consultation, they did. As soon as they were out of sight, Brant went to the corner of the house and gave a long shrill yell. Soon a small band of Mohawks were seen crossing an adjoining field with great speed. As they came up, he addressed them 'Where is your paint ? Here, put my mark on this woman.' As soon as it was done, he added, ' You are now probably safe.' " *

Great embarassment in subsisting the loyal forces in the field was felt by Col. Guy Johnson, immediately on their organization, which was assigned by him as

---

*History of Tryon Co.

a reason why he removed westward; first
to the Upper Settlements of the Mohawk
Valley, and then to Fort Stannix. The
same difficulty existed throughout the
" *Petit Guerre*" which was carried on by
the Indians under Brant. The fact was,
that for the most part, they had to pro
cure their own subsistence as best they
could; from friends, by purchase or gift,
from foes, by stratagem or force Of
course, Brant and his Indians became the
terror of the whole country, and the source
of frightful stories, of bloody massacres of
helpless women and children.

The following letter of Brant will best
exhibit his humanity, his loyalty and his
necessities ·

Tunidilla, July 6th, 1777.

Mr. Carr,

  Sir,—I understand that you are a
friend to government, with some of the

settlers at the Butternuts, is the reason of my applying to you and those people for some provisions, and shall be glad if you will send me what you can spare, no matter of what sort, for which you shall be paid, you keeping an account of the whole.

From your friend

and humble servant

JOSEPH BRANT.*

To Mr. Persofer Carr.

Under the circumstances in which Brant was placed it is not surprising if he did many things—or at least permitted them to be done—which under other circumstances he would not have permitted.

In a number of cases, which are well authenticated, he saved the lives of individuals upon recognizing them as members of the Masonic Fraternity, to which he belonged. But as he was the recognized

---

*History of Tryon Co.

leader of the Indians in all the conflicts in the Mohawk Valley and its vicinity, he was held responsible for all the exaggerated stories of devastation and cruelty which the excited state of the public mind attributed to him, and which became incorporated into the current history of the period, and have to some extent been perpetuated to the present day

CHAPTER VI.

The campaign of Gen. Sullivan against the Senecas in the fall of 1779 proved very disastrous to the Indians. Although vigorously opposed by all the available British force, both English and Indian, Sullivan penetrated into the Senecas' country, destroying their towns, and all their property, and provisions, and driving the Indians under the protection of the guns of Fort Niagara. Capt. Brant accompanied the expedition from Niagara against Gen. Sullivan ,having the immediate command of the Indians, and distinguished himself by his valor, activity and military skill.   He also signalized his humanity in saving the life of Lieut. Boyd, of the American army, who fell into the hands of the Indians at Beardstown on the Genesee river.   Lieut. Boyd was subsequently executed after the Indian fashion, by order of one of the Butlers during the absence of Brant on other duty.   The winter of 1779-80 was one of extraordinary severity.   The snow fell to the depth of eight feet over all Western New York and in Canada.   The Indians suffered greatly by sickness and destitution.   Numbers died from exposure and starvation, and the carcasses of dead animals were so numerous in the forests the next summer, as to fill the atmosphere with the pestiferous odor of their decaying bodies.   Captain Brant returned to Niagara, and took up his winter quarters with Col. Guy Johnson, the Butlers—father and son—and other officers of the

Indian Department. An incident occurred during the winter which may be mentioned as an illustration of the character of the Mohawk Chief.

Among the prisoners captured by the Indians at Cherry Valley the year before, and brought to the Senecas' country, was Miss Jane Moore, who had been redeemed from the Indians by Col. Butler, and was then residing in his family at Niagara. Capt. Wm. Powell, a son of Col. Powell (whose widow married Col. Guy Johnson after the death of his wife), becoming acquainted with her, courted and married her. Capt. Brant was present at the wedding, and although he had been for some time living with his third wife, bound only by the ties of Indian marriage, he nevertheless embraced the opportunity of having the English marriage ceremony performed, which was accordingly done by Col. Butler acting as one of the King's Commission of the Peace for Tyron County, N.Y.

Early in the Spring of 1780, we find Brant again on the war-path. He headed a small party composed partly of "Butler's Rangers" and partly of Indian Warriors, into the Mohawk Valley. The Oneida Indians, who had remained upon their lands in the Mohawk Valley, suffered some by this expedition, and Capt. Harper, of Harpersfield, with a small party were captured and carried prisoners to Niagara. Capt. Brant knew Capt. Harper well, and on recognizing him among the prisoners, rushed up to him, tomahawk in hand, and said, "Harper, I am sorry to find you here." "Why are you sorry, Capt. Brant?" "Because," rejoined Brant, "I must kill you, although we were school mates when we were boys." As scalps were much easier carried to Niagara than prisoners, the Indians were for putting the prisoners to death, but Brant's influence was exerted successfully to prevent the massacre. When they arrived at the Genessee River and encamped for the night, Capt. Brant dispatched a runner to Niagara with information of his approach, and the number of his prisoners. His friend, Capt. Powell, who married Miss Moore, the Cherry Valley captive, was at the Fort. Capt. Brant knew that Capt. Harper was uncle to Miss Moore, now Mrs. Powell, and it had been agreed in consideration of sparing their lives, that on arrival at the Fort the prisoners should go through the customary Indian ordeal of running the gauntlet. Before arriving at the Fort two Indian encampments had to be passed; but on emerging from the woods and approaching the first, what was the surprise of the prisoners and the

chagrin of their captors, at finding the
warriors absent, and their place filled by
a regiment of British soldiers. A few
Indian boys, and some old women, only
were visible and offered little violence to
the prisoners, which was quickly sup-
pressed by the soldiers. At the second
encampment nearest the Fort, they found
the warriors absent also, and their place
occupied by another regiment of troops.
Capt. Brant led his prisoners directly
through the dreaded encampments and
brought them in safety into the Fort.
The solution of this escape from the
gauntlet was, that Capt. Powell had, at
the suggestion of Capt. Brant, enticed
the warriors away to the " nine mile
landing" for a frolic, the means for hold-
ing it being furnished from the public
stores. Col. Harper was most agreeably
surprised at escaping the gauntlet with
his party, and at being met by his niece,

the wife of one of the principal officers in command of the post. Harper knew nothing of her marriage, or even of her being at Niagara, Capt. Brant having kept it a secret from Harper.

Capt. Alexander Harper was the ancestor of the "Harper Brothers" of *Harper's* *Magazine* notoriety, of New York city. Brant headed some other expeditions into the settlements in the Mohawk Valley, in one of which Capt. Jeremiah Snider and his son, of Saugerties, N. Y., with others were taken prisoners. Those prisoners were taken over the same route as Capt. Harper and his party, but did not escape as fortunately when they arrived at Niagara, as they had to run the gauntlet between long lines of Indian warriors, women and children. But their captors interposed to prevent injury Capt. Snider, in his narrative of this

event, describes Fort Niagara as a "struc-
ture of considerable magnitude, and
great strength, enclosing an area of from
six to eight acres.   Within the enclosure
was a handsome dwelling house for the
residence of the Superintendant of Indi
ans.   It was then occupied by Col. Guy
Johnson, before whom the Capt. and his
son were brought for examination.   Col.
John Butler with his rangers lay upon
the opposite side of the river."   Capt.
Snider describes Gen. Johnson as being
" a short, pussy man, about forty years of
age, of a stern, haughty demeanor, dressed
in a British uniform, powdered locks and
cocked hat, his voice harsh, and his
brogue that of a gentleman of Irish ex-
traction."   While in the guardhouse the
prisoners were visited by Capt. Brant, of
whom Capt. Snider says, " He was a
likely fellow of fierce aspect, tall and
rather spare, well spoken, and apparently

about thirty years of age." (He was actually thirty-seven.) "He wore moc cassius elegantly trimmed with beads, leggins and breech-cloth, of superfine blue; short green coat, with two silver epaulets, and a small laced, round hat. By his side hung an elegant silver-mounted cutlass, and his blanket of blue cloth, purposely dropped in the chair on which he sat to display his epaulets, was gorgeously decorated with a border of red. He asked the prisoners many questions. Indeed the object of their capture seems to have been principally for the purpose of obtaining information." Upon being informed where they were from, Capt. Brant replied, "That is my old fighting ground." In the course of the conversation Brant said to the younger Snider, "You are young, and I pity you, but for that old villain there," pointing to the father, "I have no pity."

CHAPTER VII.

The close of the season of 1780 found Capt. Brant in his old winter quarters at Fort Niagara, with Col. Butler and Col. Guy Johnson. The forces àt Niagara were stated at this time to consist of sixty British regulars, commanded by a captain · four hundred loyalists, commanded by Col. John Butler; twelve hundred Indians, including women and children, commanded by Guy Johnson and Capt. Joseph Brant. In the spring of 1781, an expedition against the revolted Oneidas, in the Mohawk Valley, was planned under the approbation of

Gen. Haldimand to be commanded by Brant, but for some unexplained reason was never executed. Vigorous incursions were kept up by small parties of loyalists and Indians during the season, sometimes under Capt. Brant, but often under the command of others. This state of things continued with varying fortunes, until the news of an agreement for the cessation of hostilities between the United States and Great Britain was received, and in March 1783 a general peace was announced.

The Mohawks, with their loyalist neighbors in the valley of the Mohawk, had fled to Canada. Their beautiful country, together with that of their brethren of the Six Nations, had been desolated by the ravages of fire and sword. Upon the first espousal of the loyal cause by the Mohawks, Sir Guy Carleton had given a pledge that they should be re-established at the expense of the Government in their former homes and possessions. This promise had been ratified in 1779 by Gen. Haldimand, then Capt. General and Commander-in-Chief in Canada. At the close of the war the Mohawks were temporarily residing on the American side of the Niagara river at what was then called " The Landing," (now called Lewiston.)

Their brethren, the Senecas offered them a portion of their lands upon Genesee river. But as Capt. Brant said " The Mohawks were determined to sink or swim with the English," the generous offer of the Senecas was declined; and the Mohawk Chief proceeded to Quebec to arrange for the settlement of his people in the Royal Dominions. A tract of land upon the Bay of Quinte was designated for their settlement. But upon the return of Capt. Brant to his people, the location was so unsatisfactory to their brethren, the Senecas, who, apprehending that their troubles with the United States were not at an end, desired their settlement nearer the Senecas' territory. Under these circumstances Capt. Brant convened a council of his people, and the country upon the "Ouse," or Grand River, was selected, lying upon both sides of that stream from its mouth upon Lake Erie to its head; which was conveyed to the Mohawks and others of the Six Nations who chose to settle there by a formal grant from the Crown. It was at this period (1783) that Capt. Brant had been charged with entertaining ambitious views similar to those of Pontiac—of combining all the principal Indian nations into one confederacy, of which he was to be Chief; and it has been suggested that his visit to England in the fall of this year was partly for the purpose of seeing how far he could depend upon the countenance or assistance of the British Government in his enterprise.

Notwithstanding he was strongly dissuaded by Sir John Johnson from this visit to England, he immediately embarked and arrived in that country early in December

A notice of his arrival in Salisbury was published in London, December 12, 1775: " Monday last, Capt. Joseph Brant, the celebrated king of the Mohawks, arrived in this city from America; and after dining with Colonel De Peister at the headquarters here, proceeded immediately to London. This extraordinary personage is said to have presided at the late grand congress of confederate Chiefs of the Indian nations in America, and to be by them appointed to the conduct, and chief command in the war which they now meditate against the United States of America. He took his departure for England immediately as that assembly broke up, and it is conjectured that his embassy to the British Court is of great importance. This country owes much to the services of Capt. Brant during the late war in America. He was educated at Philadelphia ; is a very shrewd, intelligent person, possesses great courage and abilities as a warrior, and is inviolably attached to the British nation."

His reception at the British capital was all that he could wish. He was treated with the highest consideration and distinction. Many officers of the army whom he had met in America recognized him with great cordiality.

Preliminary to his introduction to the

King, he was receiving instructions in regard to the customary ceremonies to be
observed When he was informed that
he was to salute his Majesty by dropping
on the knee and kissing the King's hand,
Brant objected to this part of the cere
mony, saying if it was a lady it would be
a pleasant and proper thing to do; but
that he being himself a king in his own
country thought it derogatory to his
dignity and contrary to his sense of pro-
priety to perform such a servile act.

The Baroness Riedesel thus speaks of
him, having met him at the provincial
court · "I saw at times the famous Indian
Chief, Capt. Brant His manners were
polished, he expressed himself with
fluency, and was much esteemed by Gen.
Haldimand: I dined once with him at
the General's. In his dress he showed
off to advantage in the half-military and

half-savage costume.   His countenance
was manly and intelligent, and his disposition mild."   Capt. Brant returned from
England early in the year 1786, having
accomplished much for his people with
the Government, and enjoyed much
social intercourse with the most distinguished society in London.   In the
grant of the land to the Mohawks, such
other of the Six Nations as were inclined
to make their settlement upon it were in-
cluded.   This led to some difficulty and
dissatisfaction, by the intrusion of individuals of the Six Nations who did not
fully sympathize with the Mohawks in
their loyalty to the British Government.
The whole weight of these difficulties
seemed to fall upon Capt. Brant; and
his friends were at one time anxious
not only for his personal safety, but also
for his popularity and influence.   But he
ably sustained and defended himself,

justifying the acts for which he had been censured, and his conduct was approved at a full Council of the Six Nations at Niagara, in presence of the agent and commanding officer.

CHAPTER VIII.

Although a treaty of peace between Great Britain and the United States had been signed, hostilities between the United States and the Indians had not ceased, and Capt. Brant, with one hundred and fifty of his Mohawk warriors, joined the forces, mostly Indians, which so signally defeated Gen. St. Clair, at or near what is now Pittsburgh.

A pacification of the Indian troubles seemed to be an object greatly desired both by the Government of Great Britain and that of the United States,

and the acknowledged ability and influ
ence of Capt. Brant was sought by both,
and led to an active and extensive correspondence with the officers and agents
of both Governments.

Early in 1792 Capt. Brant was in-
vited to visit the city of Phila
delphia, the then seat of Government
of the United States. The newspapers in New York announced his arrival
in that city in the following terms : "On
Monday last arrived in this city from his
settlement on the Grand River, on a visit
to some of his friends in this quarter,
Capt. Joseph Brant, of the British Army,
the famous Mohawk Chief, who so emi-
nently distinguished himself during the
late war, as the military leader of the Six
Nations. We are informed that he in-
tends to visit the city of Philadelphia;"
which he did in June, 1792, and was received by the President of the United

States with cordiality and respect. There is no doubt that strenuous efforts were made at this time to engage his active interposition with the Indians to bring about peace, and also to conciliate his friendship to the United States. Although nothing could divert him from his loyalty to the Government of his choice, yet the visit seems to have given mutual satisfaction to himself and the President

The Secretary of War wrote to Gen. Chapin, U. S. Superintendent of Indian affairs, as follows· "Capt. Brant's visit will, I flatter myself, be productive of great satisfaction to himself, by being made acquainted with the humane views of the President of the United States."

The Secretary also wrote to Gen. Clinton · "Capt. Brant appears to be a judicious and sensible man I flatter myself his journey will be satisfactory to himself and beneficial to the United

States." A change in the Government
of Canada about this time, creating a
separate Government for the Upper
Province, brought new men and new
measures upon the stage of action. Col. J
G. Simcoe was appointed Lieut.-Governor
of the newly organized territory. The
new Governor brought out from England
letters of introduction to the Mohawk
Chief. They became fast friends, and in
all the peace negotiations with the
Western Indians, Capt. Brant became an
active participant in the interests of the
Government of Great Britain.

The beautiful tract of country
upon the Grand River which had
been designated for the settlement
of the Mohawks, attracted the cupidity
of white men, as their equally beautiful
country in the valley of the Mohawk and
Western New York had done before; and
Capt Brant exerted his influence with his

people to induce them to exchange their hunting for agriculture. In furtherance of this idea, he conceived the plan of making sales and leases of land to skilled white agriculturists. But the Colonial Government interposed objections, claiming that the donation from Government was only a right of occupancy, and not of sale. Capt. Brant combatted this idea, but was overuled by the officers of the Government, including his friend, Gov. Simcoe. Very general dissatisfaction seems to have prevailed among the Indians in regard to the legal construction of the title to their lands, and attempts were made to negotiate a peaceful settlement of the difficulty but with indifferent success. Capt. Brant was anxious to encourage and promote the civilization of his people ; and, in his negotiations with Gen. Haldimand, stipulated for the erection of a church, which was built upon their lands upon the Grand River, and furnished with a bell and communion service, brought from their former home in the valley of the Mohawk, and is believed to be the first temple erected to the worship of Almighty God in the Province of Upper Canada.

Capt. Brant continued to be the unyielding advocate of the rights of his people as an independent nation to their lands, to the end of his life. His views, and the arguments by which he sustained them, may be gathered from an extract of a speech which he delivered at a meeting of Chiefs and Warriors at Niagara, before Col. Sheafe, Col. Claus and others, on the occasion of a government proclamation forbidding the sale and leasing of any of their lands by the Indians. "In the year 1775," said he, "Lord Dorchester, then Sir Guy Carlton, at a numerous council, gave us every encouragement, and requested us to assist in defending their country, and to take an active part in defending His Majesty's possessions, stating that when the happy day of peace should arrive, and should we not prove successful in the contest, that he would put us on the same footing in which we stood previous to joining him.   This flattering promise was pleasing to us, and gave us spirit to embark heartily in his Majesty's cause. We took it for granted that the word of so great a man, or any promise of a public nature, would ever be held sacred. We were promised our lands for our services, and these lands we were to hold on the same footing with those we fled from at the commencement of the American war ; when we joined, fought and bled in your cause. Now is published a proclamation forbidding us leasing those very lands, that were positively given us in lieu of

those of which we were the sovereigns of
the soil, of those lands we have forsaken
we sold, we leased, and we gave away,
when, and as often as we saw fit, without
hindrance on the part of your Government, for your Government well knew
we were the lawful sovereigns of the soil,
and they had no right to interfere with us
as independent nations."

CHAPTER IX.

Capt. Brant entered into an extensive correspondence with his friends. Men of distinction, both in the United States and England, principally in regard to the title of the lands of his people, and their settlement and civilization, an object which seemed to lie very near his heart. His correspondence, in relation to the settlement of a missionary at Grand River, shows that he considered it of great importance to the realization of his wishes, in regard to the moral and spiritual interests of his people. He was opposed in this matter, but finally succeeded

in procuring the settlement of the Rev
Davenport Phelps, who had married a
daughter of the Rev. Dr. Wheelock, the
early friend and preceptor of Capt. Brant.
Mr. Phelps was a graduate of Yale Col
lege, and became a missionary of the
Episcopal Chucrh in Western New York.
He was ordained in Trinity Church, New
York, in December, 1801, and immediately entered upon the active duties of a
missionary.   He had settled in the
Province of Upper Canada; his residence
being upon a farm near Burlington Bay,
at the head of Lake Ontario.   In 1805
he removed his family from Canada to
Onondaga, N. Y.

It has been already stated that Capt.
Brant was thrice married. He had two
children by his first wife, none by
the second, and seven by the third.
Isaac Brant, his eldest child, became the source of the greatest trou-

ble to him through a love of strong
drink, and while under its influence attempted the murder of his father; but in
the assault, which was made in the
presence of a large number of persons at
a public gathering, the son received a
wound, which though not dangerous,
proved fatal, by reason of excitement and
intoxication. Capt. Brant immediately
surrendered himself to the civil authorities, and resigned his commission, which
he yet retained in the British service. It
was not accepted, however. A council
of the principal Sachems and Warriors
was held; all the facts and circumstances
were considered with great deliberation;
when the following certificate of opinion
was signed unanimously and a copy delivered to Capt. Brant.

" *Brother*,—We have heard and considered your case; we sympathize with
you. You are bereaved of a beloved son.

But that son raised his parricidal hand against the kindest of fathers. His death was occasioned by his own crime. With one voice we acquit you of all blame. We tender you our hearty condolence, and may the Great Spirit above bestow upon you consolation and comfort under your affliction."

The names of his children by his third wife, in the order of their birth, were Joseph, Jacob, John, Margaret, Catharine, Mary and Elizabeth.

The education of his children seems never to have been lost sight of amid all the cares and perplexities of his public life. The following letter written by Capt. Brant to James Wheelock, son of the early President of Dartmouth College, his former preceptor in the "Moor's Charity School," will best illustrate his views on that subject·

NIAGARA, 3rd October, 1800.

DEAR SIR,—

Although it is a long time since I have had the pleasure of seeing you, still I have not forgot there is such a person in being, and now embrace the kind offer you once made me in offering to take charge of my son Joseph, whom I certainly at that time should have sent out, had it not been that there was apparently a jealousy existing between the British and Americans ; however, I hope it is not yet too late. I send both my sons, Joseph and Jacob, who I doubt not will be particularly attended to by my friends.

I could wish them to be studiously attended to, not only as to their education, but likewise to their morals in particular. This is, no doubt, needless mentioning, as I know of old, and from personal expe rience at your seminary, that these things are paid strict attention to. Let my sons be at what schools soever, your overseeing them will be highly flattering to me. I should, by this opportunity, have wrote

Mr. John Wheelock on the same subject but a hurry of business at this time prevents me. I shall hereafter take the first opportunity of dropping him a few lines. Until then, please make my best respects to him, and earnestly solicit his friendship and attention to my boys, which, be assured of, I shall ever gratefully acknowledge.

I am, Dear Sir, wishing you and your family health and happiness,

Your friend and well-wisher,

JOSEPH BRANT.

To MR. JAMES WHEELOCK.

The two boys, Jacob and Jaseph, were sent to school at Hanover, and prosecuted their studies quite to the satisfaction of their teachers, exhibiting not only excellent capacity and diligence, but good deportment, and great amiability of character. Unfortunately a difficulty sprung up between the boys, which resulted in Joseph leaving the school and returning to his parents. Jacob remained a while longer, when he too visited home ; but subsequently returned to the school to resume his studies. On the occasion of his sons return, Capt. Brant writes to his friend, Mr. James Wheelock, the following letter :

" NIAGARA, 14th December, 1802.
" MY DEAR SIR—

" I received your very polite and friendly letter by my son Jacob, and am very much obliged to you, your brother, and all friends, for the great attentions that have been paid to both of my sons, and to Capt. Dunham for the great care he took of Jacob on the journey.

"My son would have returned to you long before this but for a continued sickness in the family, which brought Mrs. Brant very low.

"My son Jacob and several of the children were very ill. My son returns to be under the care of the President, and

I sincerely hope he will pay such attention to his studies as will do credit to himself, and be a comfort to his friends. The horse that Jacob rides out, I wish to be got in good order, after he arrives, and sold, as an attentive scholar has no time to ride about. Mrs. Brant joins me in most affectionate respects to you and Mrs. Wheelock.

"I am, Dear Sir, with great respect,

"Your sincere friend

"And humble servant,

"JOSEPH BRANT."

To JAMES WHEELOCK, Esq:

The correspondence of Brant, after his retirement from military to civil life, be sides that pertaining to the current business which engaged much of his attention with literary and scientific men, was considerable. His replies to letters of this class show him to have been a man of deep reflection, independent thought, and of intelligence above most of the white men of his time, and are characterized by good common sense.

None of the sons of Capt. Brant seem to have achieved distinction, if we except John, the youngest, who succeeded to his father's title. He received, it is said, a good English education, and improved his mind by study and travel; became distinguished for his literary acquirements, fine commanding presence and polished address. His society was sought by gentlemen of the first distinction, both in Europe and America.

A few years before his death, Capt. Joseph Brant built a fine dwelling on a tract of land presented him by the British Government, at the head of Lake Ontario, occupying a fine commanding eminence, affording an extensive view of the lake and surrounding country, now called Wellington Square. Here he removed with his family, and here he closed his extraordinary and eventful life, on the 24th of November, 1807, at the age of nearly sixty-five years. His remains were interred at the Mohawk Village, on the Grand River, by the side of the Church built through his instrumentality, together with the other deceased members of his family, where a monument marks the spot, on which is inscribed the following epitaph :

" *This Tomb is erected to the memory of Thayendanegea, or Capt. Joseph Brant, principal Chief and Warrior of the Six Nations Indians, by his fellow-subjects, admirers of his fidelity and attachment to the British Crown. Born on the banks of the Ohio river, 1742. Died at Wellington Square, U.C., 1807.*

"*It also contains the remains of his son, Ahyouwaighs, or Capt. John Brant, who succeeded his father as Tekarihogea, and distinguished himself in the war of 1812 and 15. Born at the Mohawk village, U.C., 1794. Died at the same place, 1832. Erected 1850.*"

APPENDIX.

The English historian, Weld, in his " Travels through the States of North America, and the Provinces of Upper and Lower Canada, during the years 1795, 1796 and 1797," has the following notice of Capt. Brandt, page 485

'Brandt, at a very early age, was sent to a college in New England, where, being possessed of a good capacity, he soon made very considerable progress in the Greek and Latin languages.

"Uncommon pains were taken to instill into his mind the truths of the Gospel. He professed himself to be a warm admirer of the principles of Christianity, and in hopes of being able to convert his nation on returning to them he absolutely translated the Gospel of St. Matthew into the Mohawk language; he also translated the established form of prayer of the Church of England.

"Before Brandt, however, had finished his course of studies, the American war broke out, and fired with that spirit of glory which seems to have been implanted by nature in the breast of the Indian, he immediately quitted the college, repaired to his native village, and shortly afterwards, with a considerable body of his nation, joined some British troops under the command of Sir John Johnston.

"Here he distinguished himself by his valor in many different engagements, and was soon raised, not only to the rank of a war chief, but also to that of a war chief in His Majesty's service.

"It was not long, however, before Brandt sullied his reputation in the British army. A skirmish took place with a body of American troops; the action was warm, and Brandt was shot by a musket ball in the heel; but the Americans, in the end, were defeated, and an officer with about sixty men were taken prisoners. The officer, after having delivered up his sword, had entered into conversation with Col. Johnston, who commanded the British troops, and they were talking together in the most friendly manner, when Brandt, having stolen slily behind them, laid the American officer lifeless on the ground with a blow of his tomahawk. The indignation of Sir John Johnston, as may readily be supposed, was roused by such an act of treachery, and he resented it in the warmest language. Brandt listened unconcernedly, and when he had finished, told him that he was sorry what he had done had caused his displeasure, but that indeed his heel was extremely painful at the moment, and he could not help revenging himself on the only chief of the party he saw taken. Since he had killed the officer, his *heel*, he added, was much less painful to him than it had been before.

When the war broke out the Mohawks resided on the Mohawk river, in the State of New York, but on peace being made, they emigrated into Upper

Canada, and their principal village is now situated
on the Grand River, which falls into Lake Erie on
the north side, about sixty miles from the town of
Newark, or Niagara. There Brandt at present re-
sides. He has built a comfortable habitation for
himself, and any stranger that visits him may rest
assured of being well received, and of finding a
plentiful table well served every day. He has no
less than thirty or forty negroes, who attend to his
horses, cultivate his grounds, &c., &c. These poor
creatures are kept in the greatest subjection, and
they dare not attempt to make their escape, for he
has assured them, that, if they did so, he would follow
them himself, though it were to the confines of
Georgia, and would tomahawk them wherever he
met them. They know his disposition too well not
to think that he would adhere strictly to his word.

Brandt receives from Government half-pay as
Captain, besides annual presents, &c., which in all
amounts, it is said, to five hundred pounds per
annum. We had no small curiosity, as you may
well imagine, to see this Brandt, and we procured

letters of introduction to him from the Governor's Secretary, and from different officers and gentlemen of his acquaintance, with an intention of proceeding from Newark to his village.

Most unluckily, however, on the day before that of our arrival at the town of Newark, he had embarked on board a vessel for Kingston at the opposite end of the lake. You may judge of Brandt's consequence, when I tell you that a lawyer of Niagara, who crossed Lake Ontario with us from Kingston, where he had been detained for some time by contrary winds, informed us the day after our arrival at Niagara, that by his not having reached that place in time to transact some law business for Mr. Brandt, and which had consequently been given to another person, he should be the loser of one hundred pounds at least.

Brandt's sagacity led him early in life to discover that the Indians had been made the dupe of every foreign power that had gained footing in America, and indeed could he have had any doubts on the subject they would have been removed when he saw the British after having demanded and received the assistance of the Indians in the American war, so unjustly and ungenerously yield up the whole of the Indian territories east of the Mississippi and south of the lakes, to the people of the United States, the very enemies, in short, they had made to themselves at the request of the British. He perceived with regret that the Indians, by espousing the quarrels of the whites, and espousing different interests were weakening themselves, whereas, if they remained aloof, guided by one policy, they would soon become formidable, and treated with more respect. He formed the bold scheme there-fore of uniting the Indians together in one grand confederacy, and for this purpose he sent messengers to different Chiefs, proposing that a general meeting should be held of the heads of every tribe to take the subject into consideration. But certain of the tribes suspicious of Brandt's designs, and fearful that he was bent upon acquiring power for himself by this measure, opposed it with all their influence. Brandt has, in consequence, become extremely obnoxious to many of the most warlike, and with such a jealous eye do they now regard him that it would not be perfectly safe for him to return to the Upper country.

He has managed the affairs of his own people with great ability, and leased out their superfluous lands for them for long terms of years, by which measure a certain annual revenue is ensured to the nation. He wisely judged that it was much better to do so than to suffer the Mohawks, as many other tribes had done, to sell their possessions by piecemeal, the sums of money they received for which. however great, would soon be dissipated if paid to them at once. Whenever the affairs of his nation shall permit him to do so, Brandt declares it to be his intention to sit down to the study of the Greek language, of which he professes himself a great admirer, and to translate from the original into the Mohawk language more of the New Testament ; yet this same man, shortly before we arrived at Niagara, killed his own son with his own hand. The son it seems was a drunken, good-for-nothing fellow, who had often avowed his intention of destroying his father.   One evening he absolutely entered the apartment of his father and had begun to grapple with him, perhaps with a view to put his unnatural threats into execution, when Brandt drew a short sword and felled him to the ground.   Brandt speaks of this affair with regret, but at the same time without any of that emotion which another person than an Indian might be supposed to feel.   He con- soled himself for the   act   by thinking that he has benefitted the nation by ridding them of a rascal. Brandt wears his hair in the Indian style, and also the Indian dress. Instead of the wrapper or blanket he wears a short coat such as I have described, similar to a hunting frock."

APPENDIX.

The following is an extract from the history of Schohorié County, page 220 :

It appears that in July 1778, Joseph Brant had then with some eighty warriors commenced his marauding enterprises on the settlements at Unadilla, by appropriating their cattle, sheep and swine to his own benefit. To obtain satisfaction for those cattle, and if possible to get the Indians to remain neutral in the approaching contest, Gen. Herkimer in the latter part of June, with three hundred and eighty of the Tryon County militia proceeded to Unadilla (an Indian settlement on the Susquehanna River) to hold an interview with Brant. That celebrated Chief then at Oquago, was sent for by Gen. Herkimer, and arrived on the 27th, after the Americans had been there about eight days waiting.

Col. John Harper who attended Gen. Herkimer at this time, made an affidavit on the 16th of July following the interview, showing the principal grievances of which the Indians complained, as also the fact that they were in covenant with the King, whose belts were yet lodged with them, and whose service they intended to enter.

The instrument further testified that Brant instead of returning to Oswego as he had informed Gen. Herkimer was his intention, had remained in the neighborhood on the withdrawal of the Ameri can Militia, and was proposing to destroy the frontier settlements.

The following relating to the interview between Gen. Herkimer and Brant is obtained from the venerable Joseph Wagner, of Fort Plain. He states that at the first meeting of Gen. Herkimer with Brant, the latter was attended by three other Chiefs, William Johnson, a son of Sir William Johnson by Molly Brant, which son was killed at the battle of Oriskany the same year. But, a smart looking fellow, with curly hair, supposed to be part Indian and part Negro, and a short dark skinned Indian.

The four were encircled by a body guard of some twenty noble looking warriors. When in his presence Brant rather haughtily asked Gen. Herkimer the object of his visit, which was readily made known. But seeing so many attendants, the Chief suspected the interview was sought for another purpose.

Said Brant to Gen. Herkimer, I have five hundred warriors at my command, and can in an instant destroy you and your party ; but we are old neighbors and friends, and I will not do it. Col. Cox, a young officer who accompanied Gen. Herkimer exchanged several sarcastic remarks with Brant, which served not a little to irritate him and his followers. The two had a quarrel a few years previous about lands around the upper Indian Castle. Provoked to anger, Brant asked Cox if he was not the " son-in-law of old George Clock ?" " Yes," replied Cox in a tone of malignity, " and what is that to you, you d—d Indian."

At the close of this dialogue, Brant's guard ran off to their camp firing several guns and making the hills echo back their savage yells. Gen. Herkimer assured Brant that he intended his visit for one of a pacific character and urged him to interpose to prevent anything of a hostile nature. A word from Brant hushed the tumult of passion, which a moment before threatened serious consequences. The parties, however, were too much excited to proceed with the business which had convened them. Brant, addressing Gen. Herkimer, said, it is needless to multiply words at this time ; I will meet you here at precisely nine o'clock to-morrow morning. The parties then separated to occupy their former position in camp. They again met on the 28th of June. Brant was the first to speak. " Gen. Herkimer," said he, " I now fully comprehend the object of your visit; but you are too late, I am engaged to serve the King. We are old friends, and I can do no less than to let you return unmolested, although you are in my power." After a little more conversation, of a friendly nature, the parties agreed to separate amicably. The conference ended, Gen. Herkimer presented to Brant seven or eight fat cattle that had just arrived, owing to obstructions on the outlet of Otsego lake, down which stream they were driven or transported. For three days before the arrival of the cattle, the Americans were on short allowance. It is said that at this second interview of Brant with Gen. Herkimer, the latter had taken the precaution to privately select four reliable men, in case any symptoms of treachery should be exhibited, to shoot down Brant and his Chiefs at a given signal, but no occasion to execute these precautionary measures occurred.

The following anecdote is related of Brant as occurring in connection with the capture of prisoners at Cherry Valley. Among the captures made by him at that place was a man named Vrooman with whom he had been formerly acquainted. He concluded to give Vrooman his liberty, and after they had proceeded several miles, he sent Vrooman back about two miles alone, ostensibly to procure some birch bark, expecting, of course, to see no more of him. After several hours Vrooman came hurrying back with the bark, which the Captain no more wanted than he did a pair of goggles. Brant said he sent his prisoner back on purpose to afford him an opportunity to escape, but he was so big a fool he did not know it, and that consequently he was compelled to take him along to Canada.

The history of Schoharie County, page 334, contains the following note :

" In person Brant was about middling size, of a square, stout build, fitted rather for enduring hardships than for quick movements. His complexion was lighter than that of most Indians, which resulted perhaps from his less exposed manner of living. This circumstance probably gave rise to a statement which has been often repeated, that he was of mixed origin. The old people in the Mohawk Valley, to whom he was known generally, agree that he was not a full blood Indian, but was part white.

" He was married in the winter of 1779 to a daughter of Col. Croghan, by an Indian woman. The circumstances of this marriage are somewhat singular. He was present at the wedding of Miss Moore, from Cherry Valley, who had been brought away a prisoner, and who married an officer of the garrison of Fort Niagara. Brant had lived with his wife for some time previous according to the Indian custom without marriage, but now insisted that the marriage ceremony should be performed. This was accordingly done by Col. Butler who was still considered a Magistrate. After the war he removed with his nation to Canada. There he was employed in transacting important business for his tribe. He went out to England after the war, and was honorably received there. Joseph Brant died on the 24th November, 1807, at his residence near the head of Lake Ontario, in the 65th year of his age. Not long before that event the British Government refused for the first time to confirm a sale of lands made by him, which mortified him exceedingly The sale was afterwards confirmed, at which he was so much elated that he got into an excitement that is said to have laid the foundation of his sickness.

" The wife of Brant who was very dignified in her appearance, would not converse in English before strangers, notwithstanding she could speak it fluently."

CPSIA information can be obtained
at www.ICGtesting.com
Printed in the USA
LVOW13s2124151216
517504LV00006B/590/P

9 781331 907602